Some things don't change—the enemy is still a liar and still uses debt to enslave Christians.

This little book is as timely today as it was when it was first published in 1982. I pray that it will be a blessing and set you free to be all God wants you to be.

Love,

Norma Bixler

Norma Bixler
January 2012

"All my adult life I had worried about money. Suddenly, I wasn't worrying anymore, although my personal debts were as large as ever. Because I was no longer worrying about my finances, God was free to work the miracle I needed. I had gotten out of His way.

"In less than 90 days, my seminary debt was completely paid! All my other bills were paid, too! And, for the first time since we were married, Norma and I were totally out of debt! In less than three months!"

Russ Bixler
1982

LEARNING TO KNOW GOD AS PROVIDER

RUSSELL BIXLER

WHITAKER
HOUSE

LEARNING TO KNOW GOD AS PROVIDER

2012 Commemorative Reprint for:
Cornerstone TeleVision
1 Signal Hill Drive
Wall, PA 15148

ISBN: 978-0-88368-120-6
Printed in the United States of America
© 1982 by Western Pennsylvania Christian Broadcasting Co.

Whitaker House
1030 Hunt Valley Circle
New Kensington, PA 15068
www.whitakerhouse.com

Credits:
Text Artwork by Waltraud Hendel
Layout by Hellen Mierski
Typesetting by Jean Stewart
Cover artwork by Mary Anne Skeba

4 5 6 7 8 9 10 11 **UH** 17 16 15 14 13 12

Contents

Foreword

I have known Russ Bixler and his lovely wife, Norma, for many years. When I first met them they were located in a small church in Pittsburgh and were yet trying to believe God for a great charismatic rally for thousands of people in Western Pennsylvania, and then Russ dared to believe God for even greater things including a television channel to serve the Pittsburgh area.

There is no question that Russ has met God as a provider, and approaches this subject not as a theoretician but as one who has been tested in the fires of experience.

Pat Robertson

Preface

I discovered a long time ago just how God uses me as a teacher of the Bible. Or at least how He uses me when I teach biblical principles for living.

First, He allows me to live through a particular experience—sometimes a blessed experience, sometimes a painful one. Then He directs me to the scriptures that explain what is happening to me, and, most important, to those scriptures that help me learn to profit from the situation. If it's a pleasant experience, the Lord will show me how to share that blessing with others. If it's a troubled experience, He likewise shows me—always from the Bible—how to help others in similar difficulties.

This may surprise you, but the Bible is not a book of theology. Rather, scripture tells of real people, real incidents in actual lives—and how God acted mightily in all those lives. The Bible is quite personal and most practical!

This book is intensely personal, too. It's chock full of intimate pictures of our lives, Norma's and mine together. The narratives are presented honestly and plainly. Some of it is tragedy, but more—lots more—is triumph. This is true only because Norma and I have discovered that *God is on our side!*

He's on *your* side, too! God is still acting mightily in the lives of His people!

If you have experienced great difficulty in paying your bills, this book is for you.

LEARNING TO KNOW GOD AS PROVIDER

Chapter 1

A Spirit of Poverty Takes Control

"You shall remember the Lord your God, for it is He who gives you power to get wealth. Beware lest you say in your heart, 'My power and the might of my hand have gotten me this wealth'"(Deuteronomy 8:18, 17).

The wild spending spree of the last fifty years has almost ended. The irresponsible generation to which I belong has long since mortgaged its children's future, and that of its grandchildren as well—never recognizing that the only similarity between God and the Government is that both begin with the same letter of the alphabet.

Now we must begin living together again—caring, loving, assisting—letting God be God and letting the Church be the Church. Depending once again upon the God my generation tried to walk away from.

Several weeks ago I sensed the Spirit of God gently informing me that it's time to tell this very personal story.

I was raised during what has been labeled the "Great Depression" of the 1930's. I recall my dad's being unable to work for a year-and-a-half because of an injured shoulder. Dad could always find a job—any job—but his pain-wracked body wouldn't permit it. We didn't know the Lord Jesus who "took our infirmities and bore our diseases."

Dad had known "hard times." He was born in a one-room, dirt-floor log cabin. So our family's economic problem was not the widespread unemployment. Rather, our problem was the *spirit* that pervaded the nation. Let me explain.

Everyone talked so much about "the depression." The news media would feature any politician who wanted to bring up the subject. I remember poor people walking back alleys, peering hopefully into garbage cans for scraps of food. Many banks were failing because of depositors' fears causing them to withdraw their savings. Great numbers of people lost their homes as large city banks foreclosed mercilessly. Men walked the streets looking for work. Hoboes multiplied among the young and rootless.

I recall the indignation I felt the morning I walked to the store, clutching a nickel and three pennies in my little hand, intending to purchase a quart of milk, only to hear the grocer announce apologetically, "Milk has gone up to nine cents." I knew what hunger felt like, and I hated it. The first song I remember was "Happy Days Are Here Again." Bands were playing the song again and again, but it only echoed, hollow and unfulfilling, across the land.

You see, in those days we thought poor, we talked poor, we acted poor, we lived poor, and so we *were* poor. Thomas Carlyle once said, "A man is what he thinks about all day." And, cumulatively, a *nation* is what it thinks about all day. Literally, our speech and our thoughts made us poor. Much poorer than we had to be! As I said earlier, there was a *spirit* that had captured our country.

Now, when the world talks about a "spirit," it means an impersonal, nebulous awareness that sweeps over the populace. But when the Bible talks about a "spirit," it means much more. In the Bible, a spirit (not the Holy Spirit) is a personality— someone evil—bringing pain, bondage or, perhaps, even death. Don't be so blind as to deny the reality of evil spirits (or demons) simply because you can't see them. Since the Bible proves true in real life, this book will always deal with *reality*, and not what so-called "modern" man might *wish* reality to be.

"The thief comes only to steal and destroy; I came that they might have life, and have it abundantly" (John 10:10).

Ever since the advent of "rationalism" a couple of centuries ago, intellectual man has

15

de-supernaturalized our culture. No angels, no demons, no miracles, and finally, no God! And so, because modern man chooses to deny the entire, controlling realm of the supernatural, most people in our nation tend to live in an unreal world. How ironic that modern psychologists can describe so accurately the *behavior* of demons in psychotic people, and yet never admit (publicly) that demons are the very cause of that perverse behavior! Humanistic psychologists excuse themselves by saying they don't understand the dynamics underlying mental illness.

Jesus knew all about evil spirits. Dealing with demons occupied fully one-third of His ministry as recorded in the gospels. Christians for centuries have known about evil spirits. Today Christians worldwide are learning once again how to deal—in power—with the devil's messengers. Let's see how evil spirits operate.

Sin invites demons. Sin allows them to gain entrance. First, evil spirits tempt people. For example, a young accountant finds himself in financial difficulty. He also notices an opportunity to embezzle company funds without being caught. After all, the company doesn't pay him what he's worth, so, "I'll just take little amounts from time to time to make certain I receive what I'm worth. They don't appreciate how hard I work here!"

Soon this accountant will find himself embezzling larger amounts, and doing it more frequently—whether he needs it or not. He can't help himself. He has given a lying spirit the lordship over an important part of his life. His lying spreads to other areas. After several years, he becomes almost unable to distinguish the truth from a lie. By that time, we could actually say that he lies because he can no longer help himself.

"...Each person is tempted when he is lured and enticed by his own desire. Then desire when it has conceived gives birth to sin; and sin when it is full-grown brings forth death" (James 1:14, 15). Read also Romans 1:21-32.

This is not science fiction, nor is it superstition: it's real. Truth in the Kingdom of God is quite different from what this world calls truth. Of course, Christians can be released from such demonic oppression. So don't let the mention of demons frighten you.

Many of our English translations of the New Testament use the expression, "demon possessed." This is tragic, for there is no basis in the original Greek for such a translation. The actual word in the Greek is "demonized," which could mean "oppressed" or "afflicted" by an evil spirit. "My daughter is severely possessed by a demon," reads the Revised Standard Version of Matthew 15:22. The King James Version of Mark 1:32 tells of "them that were possessed by devils."

17

The word "possessed" is an improper choice, and it puts undue fear in Christians. Jesus had power over evil spirits, and He bestowed upon us that same authority: He "gave them power and authority over all demons...." (Luke 9:11). Later, the seventy disciples returned with joy: "Lord, even the demons are subject to us in your name!" (Luke 10:17). The name of Jesus is powerful! "He who is in you is greater than he who is in the world" (1 John 4:4).

When the Lord said He came to set us free, He meant much more than we normally realize. And that leads me to the point of this book. *Jesus came to set us free from the demon of poverty!*

This particular evil spirit captured a large number of Americans in my generation. Fifty years ago our nation seemed to stop looking to God; somehow the proper fiscal management by the Federal Government was going to solve our economic problems. The spirit of poverty tells lies to its victims. This demon led our whole nation into sin. Depression-ridden Americans invited the evil spirit into themselves by the sin of not trusting God for their prosperity. That's right—it really was sin. Most of us did not trust God for our physical needs. All the New Deal economics of the 1930's had little effect on the nationwide affliction. My generation— for the first time in America's history—decided that Government should do those things which only God is able to do. The government, we thought, should be able to provide all the economic answers. Today we are reaping the painful harvest of that sin.

Finally, after years of agony, World War II brought the country into an artificial prosperity, a tragic "cure" whose financial impact was to catch up with America years later. Americans of my generation still suffer terribly from this spirit of poverty. Witness the behavior of aging labor union leaders who can never squeeze enough money out of the employers; witness the nationwide "depression-phobia" among the middle-aged and elderly; witness the mania among those over forty to accumulate material possessions far beyond their needs; witness the irrational bitterness among the heirs to their parents' estates; witness the unnecessary affluence of well-to-do American suburbia. These are all outward marks of the inner workings of the spirit of poverty.

So a spirit of poverty—living, evil, binding—took up residence within me also. Children often inherit demons. I picked it up from my parents who were infected before me. Norma too. She got it from her parents as well. Norma and I were in financial trouble the day we got married, primarily because we were both oppressed by a demon of poverty. And we didn't know it. Norma and I actually became everything we worried about.

"You will know the truth and the truth will make you free" (John 8:32).

19

Just what does a spirit of poverty do in a person? Simply, more of the same. It has the effect of "locking in" the poverty we are already experiencing. Even after prosperous times return, prosperity seems to be only temporary. When a spirit of poverty afflicts, the suffering human being remains financially insecure. He can never, ever, earn enough money, no matter how much wealth comes his way. Observe with me the incident I experienced some years ago.

I was preaching in a Presbyterian church, and for a reason I didn't understand at the moment, I drifted off my subject briefly. I began to explain how a man who is suffering from a spirit of poverty might earn $50,000 a year, but invariably needs $51,000 to pay his bills. As I spoke the word "fifty," my tongue seemed to get twisted, and it came out "sixty"! I wondered momentarily why I said "sixty" instead of "fifty"; but having made the mistake, I continued by adding, "And he needs $61,000 to pay his bills."

The church was full that evening, and a professional man was seated on a folding chair at the rear wall. At the conclusion of the service, he burst up the side aisle and seized my hand: "Russ! I've got to talk to you—now!"

I discovered once again how God can use a sermon when the preacher doesn't even realize it. This professional man was ashen, almost panicky. "Russ! Last year I earned $60,000! And last week I had to borrow $900 to make the final payment on my income tax!" And then I realized the awesome sovereignty of God, who had caused my tongue to say "sixty thousand" instead of "fifty thousand."

Instantly, I knew this man as if God had told me his life story. "You were born poor, weren't you?"

"Yes!" And his voice trembled.

"And you determined as a child that when you grew up, you would get a good education and work hard and never be poor again." The response came as an agonized wail.

"Now you're making all this money, and you *still* don't have enough, do you?" The man seemed almost at the point of collapse. I continued: "And if you have children, they don't understand your feelings about money. You're always reminding them of the value of the dollar."

His agony suddenly turned to a sense of excitement. Together we were on the trail of the solution to a detective mystery. "Do you know that my teenage daughter was laughing at me just the other day: 'Oh, Daddy, you worry about money all the time!'"

Then he realized his plight anew. "But what can I do about it?"

"Well," I continued. "You have a spirit of poverty. As long as that spirit is in you, you'll never be able to earn enough money." After waiting a moment for that to sink in, I told him how to get rid of this demon. "You are proud of how much money you earn. You think, 'I worked hard for all that money!'"

"You know—I do!" he interrupted. "I brag to myself about how hard I work and all the money I receive!"

"And you forget that God is your Provider," I continued. "From now on you must thank *God*—not yourself—for every penny you receive....And also, are you tithing to the Lord's work?"

"Well, I try. But I can't seem to be able to afford it."

"That's part of your answer, too. You've got to tithe." I prayed with him, but he was still a severely-shaken Christian when he walked away. All of which illustrates how a person—Christian and non-Christian alike—who is suffering the affliction of a demon of poverty can never earn enough money.

Several years later, I was speaking at a meeting in the same part of the nation. A man whose face appeared familiar approached me before the service, grinning triumphantly. As he introduced himself, I recalled that professional man whose life the finger of God so spectacularly touched. "Russ, you'll never believe it!...Oh yes, you will! Of course you will!...God has turned my finances around! I'm tithing now! I'm supporting my church and other Christian work as well! I have all the money I need, and I can hardly give it away! God has blessed me so much! Thanks for being a part of it! Praise the Lord!"

Praise the Lord indeed! I had no trouble understanding this professional man. I had been just like him in that one major respect. I too had been afflicted with a spirit of poverty.

"Great is the Lord, who delights in the welfare of His servant!" (Psalms 35:27).

God had called me to go to seminary during the 1950's, and He'd promised to provide for all our financial needs. However, I was utterly unable to believe Him, and thus I spent those seminary years—broke. Yet God was faithful to His word: we never missed a meal during those three years. He did what He said He would do.

But, oh! it was drudgery. I worried and worried and worried about money. Of course, that isn't God's way. He wanted better for my family—much better. I was merely interfering, obstructing the Lord's plans by all that worrying. I was living in sin and didn't even know it. For I was suffering from a spirit of poverty. And Norma didn't know how to help because she had one, too.

Chapter 2

Freed From Poverty

"If the Son makes you free, you will be free indeed" (John 8:36).

I graduated from seminary with a sizable debt over my head. After being called to Pittsburgh as pastor of the Church of the Brethren, I discovered that the congregation couldn't pay me enough to live on. Or at least that's what I thought. I would pay five dollars a month on this bill and ten dollars a month on that bill. And the seminary debt just hung over my head, hardly being scratched, as during many months I could only make the interest payments. Every time we started to catch up just a little, something expensive would wear out, and down into the pits of financial despair I sank again! A man with a spirit of poverty can *never earn enough money.*

Shopping for clothes was always a crisis for Norma. The clothing was no problem—*it was spending the money* that wounded her every time.

She always came back from downtown feeling guilty, apologizing to me for having bought every item, explaining in detail each bit of clothing she got at a sale price. And I hadn't spoken a critical word!

One day Norma came home from shopping looking radiant. She was excited and happy! She was even more than that: Norma just bubbled with joy. "Let me tell you what God did for me this afternoon! I was on the escalator in Horne's, between the third and fourth floors, all worried and frantic about spending money for the children's clothing. And God spoke to me! There! On the escalator!

"The Lord said, 'Don't you know that I love those children more than you do? I can provide for them if you will stop worrying about the cost.' And Russell! Something left me at that moment—there on the escalator! It was a spirit of poverty! God set me free from the spirit of poverty! It's gone! I'm free!"

"What are you talking about?" I argued. "There's no such thing as a spirit of poverty!"

"Oh yes, there is! And now I'm free from it! Oh, praise the Lord! Praise the Lord!" And she danced a little jig in front of me.

"You sound ridiculous!"

"No, I don't! Hallelujah! I had a spirit of poverty and God set me free from it! And what's more, *you've got one, too!* Lord Jesus! Set Russell free also!"

"Aw, come on, Norma. That sounds weird!"

She just ignored me, prancing around the front hall of the parsonage—free! Then Norma got bolder: "Now, I want you to ask some of our friends to pray for *you* to get rid of *your* spirit of poverty. And if you don't ask them, I will!"

"I'm sure glad *one* of us has a sense of financial responsibility!" And I stalked off.

The next Sunday, Norma gathered up a few trusted prayer warriors in the church and surrounded me. Oh! Was I embarrassed! "Russell has a spirit of poverty, and I want you all to pray for him."

They looked at me. "I think this is silly!" I responded. "Well, okay, go ahead and pray—just in case she might be right." They prayed for me, but they didn't seem too enthusiastic about it: they were afraid of offending me.

Norma did it again the following Sunday. More prayer for "Russell's spirit of poverty." But by this time, the Spirit of God was beginning to work in my heart, and I was thinking that maybe...just possibly...perhaps...could it really be?...I might have a little, tiny demon lurking somewhere in the recesses of my soul?

Several Sundays I received prayer to be delivered, but each time I felt nothing. Yet, I had to admit that Norma was different. For a few weeks I was fearful that she would be running up some outrageous clothing bills, but she hadn't spent any

27

money at all! "I'm free!" she rejoiced. "I'm free from the spirit of poverty! Praise the Lord!" And that's the way it went.

"I will deliver you out of the hand of the wicked" (Jeremiah 15:21).

One day, as I was seated at the desk in my study, I was pondering all that Norma had been preaching to me. "Lord, do I really have a spirit of poverty?"

This time the Spirit of God broke His silence. He spoke so clearly in my heart: "You always complain whenever you receive any money. You place a value on your services, and you complain if you receive less than that amount. Don't you know that *I* am your Provider?"

I wanted to crawl in a crack in the floor. I felt like Adam and Eve—naked before the Lord. A sense of guilt went through me. But God wasn't finished with me yet. He "poured it on"! "From now on I want you to praise Me for every penny you get—no matter how little it is!" And that was that!

I felt humiliated. The Holy Spirit was correct, of course. But I defended myself by insisting that I had a right to complain! "After all, I get cheated out of money I should be receiving! Well, Lord! Don't I? People cheat preachers all the time! You know that, Lord!" No answer. I could argue with Him as long as I cared to, but I knew His word was absolute truth.

Stark, simple truth!

I resigned myself to trying to implement God's instruction. I knew it wouldn't be easy, especially since my heart wasn't in it. "I've got to have some help if I'm going to do what God says."

So I told Norma what the Lord had instructed me. She beamed. Then I added, "From now on, I'm going to bring home whatever money I receive; and together you and I are going to lay our hands on it and thank the Lord." Norma had no trouble agreeing to that proposal. She knew something exciting was about to occur.

The next paycheck was lovingly surrounded by our four hands, and we praised the Lord for it. Still, nothing happened. My debts were as big as ever. Then the tests began. I was invited to speak in Indiana. I caught a plane and addressed the meeting. Afterward they gave me a check for *thirty dollars*. "Thirty dollars! I've got to pay for that plane ticket! Why, those cheap...! uh...well, uh...oh, praise the Lord!"

When I got home, I folded the thirty dollar check and told Norma to lay her hands on it with me and thank the Lord. She asked, "How much is it?"

"Don't ask!" I blurted out. "Just praise the Lord!" And Norma never asked again.

But we persisted. We praised the Lord for every penny—for every paycheck, for every honorarium from weddings, funerals, speaking engagements, even for money we were paid for selling someone a

29

few postage stamps. Still, I was broke.

I had received an invitation to speak for three consecutive evenings at a church near Pittsburgh. It was close enough that I could commute from home. At the end of the third service, I was talking with several of the church members. A man quietly slipped an envelope into my coat pocket. I assumed that he was the church treasurer and he was giving me an honorarium for speaking those three evenings. After a few more goodbyes, I got in the car and began driving home. I wasn't more than a block from the church when I heard that familiar voice in my heart: "Stop the car and open the envelope!"

"Well, Lord, Norma and I will praise you for it after I get home, and then I'll look at it." I had learned that it was easier to praise Him before I found out "how much I had been taken advantage of." The spirit of poverty truly brings a bitter quality into a person's life.

Again the voice spoke in my heart: "Stop the car and open that envelope!"

"Okay, Lord, if that's what you want." I pulled off the road at the first opportunity. After turning on the light in the car, I opened the envelope. I held in my hand a check for an odd amount. Then I suddenly realized that the congregation had given me the entire offering for all three evenings! It was at least *double* what I thought my services were worth.

The words burst from my lips: "Praise the Lord! Oh, praise you! Praise you, Lord!" There was nothing forced about *these* praises. The thanksgiving just flowed.

Suddenly, I felt something strange moving up my legs—on the inside! It went up through my body, my head, and out the roof of the car! I knew exactly what it was—it was that miserable, robbing spirit of poverty! I felt so clean and free! I was free at last! I laughed and cried and praised the Lord all the way home. "Hallelujah! I'm free!"

As long as that spirit of poverty dwelt within me, I could not identify it. I had no idea what it felt like. That spirit was almost a part of me. I may not have known what it was, but I certainly knew when it wasn't. The freedom from financial fear is wonderful! Norma and I actually shouted for joy that night. We had a midnight praise meeting! We hoped we weren't disturbing the neighbors, although I guess we were so happy we didn't even notice. God had set us both free from the spirit of poverty!

Now I was able to trust God for my material needs. All my adult life I had worried about money. Suddenly, I wasn't worrying any longer, although my personal debts were as large as ever.

Because I was no longer worrying about my finances, God was now free to work the miracle I needed. I had gotten out of His way. Within less than 90 days, my seminary debt was completely paid! Every penny of it! All the other bills were paid, too. And, for the first time since we were married,

Norma and I were totally out of debt! In less than three months! Praise the Lord!

Having an analytical mind as I do, I tried to figure out how God did that miracle. Other than that one large offering, my income remained about the same. It was baffling. I could not "put my finger" on how it happened. I had always thought that in order to get out of debt, I would need more money. However, I slowly began to perceive that God could "stretch" our income. I finally had to concede something I never like to admit: I simply could not figure it out. It still remains a mystery to me—a joyful mystery, to be sure.

He is the same God—the God of Moses—to whose credit it could be declared to the Israelites after 40 years in the desert, "Your clothing did not wear out upon you, and your sandals did not wear off your feet." How awesome to realize afresh that He who worked that miracle 3500 years ago is still manifesting the same power today!

Chapter 3

Why Pray When You Can Worry?

"Therefore I tell you, do not be anxious about your life, what you shall eat or what you shall drink, nor about your body, what you shall put on. Is not life more than food, and the body more than clothing?" (Matthew 6:25).

Jesus gives us excellent directives in the Sermon on the Mount (Matthew 5-7). They are so clear. Large portions of His discourse deal with our physical needs. "When you pray...," Jesus says in Matthew 6:5, and then He gives us rules for prayer. Then He talks some more about physical possessions, and adds one of the most important messages the world has ever heard about "worry."

Take a couple of minutes now to read Matthew 6:25-34. Then ponder it. Re-read it later, but this time read all of Matthew 6.

Begin today to pray about your finances in a new way. Pray *in peace...peaceably...*without anxiety...no fear...trusting...secure in the arms of an

Almighty God who loves you. Prayer for your physical needs should be a normal and peaceable aspect of life.

"Have no anxiety about anything, but in everything by prayer and supplication with thanksgiving make your requests known to God. And the peace of God, which passes all understanding, will keep your hearts and minds in Christ Jesus" (Philippians 4:6,7).

My grandmother repeatedly told Norma and me that "it is a sin to worry." "Grammy" didn't talk much, but what she said often packed a wallop: "It is a sin to worry." She loved Jesus, and Jesus honored her refusal to worry. A few weeks ago, Grammy died at the age of 102—healthy until her heart just stopped!

Worry is man's message to God: "I will handle this problem myself." That's right! When we are worrying, we are telling God that we can take care of ourselves without His help. That's what financial desperation is—worry. So God will step back and allow worrying man to take care of himself. The Lord never forces Himself on us; He only "stands at the door and knocks." If we invite Him into any particular area of our lives, then He is free to assert His miracle-working power in that area. I have often stated in sermons that if *I* had been God in the Garden of Eden, I would have placed a ten-foot-high electric fence around the tree of the knowledge of good and evil. But God has always remained "optional"—we can take Him or leave Him. Adam and Eve chose to leave Him.

Satan however is different, as we all know. He is constantly trying to force himself upon us. The devil brings sickness and hate and violence and fear. The Lord works with great yet gentle power—persuasive, loving, peaceable and upbuilding. But since Jesus comes to us so gently, we His servants must *practice* trusting Him in every area of our lives.

"Do you not know that God's kindness is meant to lead you to repentance?" (Romans 2:4).

Norma and I realized that we had been able to trust Jesus for our *health*, but not for our *finances*. And we hadn't even noticed it! So many of God's children have the same problem concerning their finances, and, like me, they will deny it. Because the spirit of poverty is so "sneaky," most people are as offended as I was by the truth. We hate to admit that there might be something evil in us. The spirit of poverty feels very much a part of the person afflicted with it. We actually believe that this demon is our "sense of financial responsibility." And the worst part of it is that we are thereby living in sin! We need to repent!

I can only share this truth with you. If these real-life incidents sound a little like your own personal history, then you too are suffering from this spirit of poverty. It's so easy to be freed—if you will set a discipline for yourself and stick to it. "Resist the devil and he will flee from you" (James 4:7). Some of us, however, enjoy worrying and complaining. We get a morbid pleasure out of being negative. And the whole family suffers because of that sin.

"He who conceals his transgressions will not prosper, but he who confesses and forsakes them will obtain mercy" (Proverbs 28:13).

I had not thought of this repentance as a set of rules, but that's what it is. We could call them "the laws of prosperity." One evening Norma and I were awakened to this fact by another specific word from the Lord. I was speaking at a Full Gospel Businessmen's dinner in Ohio, and the Lord was working some delightful miracles of healing. Suddenly, I felt that Norma had a word for us, and I called on her without warning. Norma stood up, having no idea of what she was to say. Slowly the words began to flow: "The Lord says there are men here tonight who are worrying about their finances. He wants you to be free from the worry, and to have all the money you need."

She continued, "God wants you to remember and observe three rules of prosperity. First, you must tithe, give ten percent of your income to the

Lord's work.

"Second, you are complaining about high prices as inflation is running wild. God is angry about your attitude. For by this complaining, you are asserting that He is not able to provide for your needs. Besides, you are only spreading gloom and doom in the stores where you shop.

"Third, you are complaining about your income. You blame your employer or your customers for not paying you what you think your services are worth. But your employer is not your provider. God is. And He's angry about that attitude also. You should be thanking God for your income, not complaining about it."

When Norma sat down, she said to me quietly, "That was the Lord! I had no idea what I was going to say when you called on me!" We both realized that she had spoken quite a word of wisdom. Perhaps we could call it a "divine mouthful." Her words ministered meaningfully to many at the meeting. Several young men were wiping tears from their cheeks. After that, Norma and I began to incorporate those three rules into our ministry whenever God would lead us to teach on the subject of a Christian and his finances.

Tithing alone is not enough. I had tithed for years without very significant results. There was some good, but it was not especially noticeable. I was violating the other two laws of prosperity because of the bitterness that ugly spirit of poverty had placed in my heart. My complaints were negating most of the positive effects of my tithing. All three principles of prosperity are essential; try neglecting just one of them and watch what happens.

To repeat,

(1) Give a tenth of your earnings to the Lord;

(2) Do not complain about high prices;

(3) Praise the Lord for all your income.

For years Norma and I had been taking a few moments before meals to thank the Lord for His provision. Occasionally, I wondered whether a Christian homemaker ever protested, "Why thank God for this food? I'm the one who prepared it!"

But I've never heard my wife protest like that. She too always joins in the thanksgiving. Yet we who are breadwinners seem to take credit ourselves for the money we earn. Husbands need to learn a lesson from our wives: If they can thank the Lord for meals they have prepared, we men can thank Him for the money we earn.

Chapter 4

The First Rule

"Bring the full tithes into the storehouse, that there may be food in my house; and thereby put me to the test, says the Lord of hosts, if I will not open the windows of heaven for you and pour down for you an overflowing blessing" (Malachi 3:10).

Norma and I had endured one brief but painful lesson in tithing during the five or six years we lived without a salary. One year, shortly after the Christmas holidays, we began to experience an intense shortage of money. We continued praising the Lord for all our income, and we made certain that we were giving the required ten percent of our income to the Lord's work. Still the debts began to pile up, continuing through February and March. I was beginning to be troubled, praying about the problem and wondering what was wrong. God had always been faithful, and now He seemed to be letting us down.

In early April, I began to work on the previous

year's income tax return. I hadn't gotten far in my calculations before I knew that something was wrong. I started adding the figures again, but the totals were the same. "But this can't be!" I protested to myself. "These totals show that we only gave 8½ percent of our income to the Lord's work last year!" We hadn't even been *close* to the full tithe! To this day, I still don't know how we missed it.

So I checked the totals once more. I'd always been so careful about giving not only the tithe, but more. In my spirit, the tithe seemed to be legalism, but *more* than the tithe always brought a sense of freedom. To make matters worse, I had to borrow more money to complete my payments on the previous year's estimated tax.

I don't think God was being capricious, or that He was punishing us. God's blessings are automatic, and the reverse is just as true. It's what we could call a universal law, operating much like the law of gravity. When we obey the law of gravity, we remain safe; if we violate it, we can get hurt. The difference is that God's spiritual laws usually work out more slowly—but just as surely. Our previous year's violation of His law of prosperity certainly worked against us within a matter of months.

"Now I've got to borrow *more* money," I grieved to myself. So I praised the Lord as before and went to the bank to get the full limit of my credit. Making up delinquent tithes is really difficult. But we did it.

And within one month every bill was paid! Only one month! Another miracle! Praise the Lord who is so faithful to fulfill His promises!

"You shall tithe all the yield of your seed...that you may learn to fear the Lord your God always" (Deuteronomy 14:22,23).

A few days ago, I received an anguished letter from a viewer of our Christian television station. He began abruptly:

"I am about at the end of my rope. I have been trusting God to meet our need for a car for four months....It just seems every avenue we've pursued has turned into a blind alley. The Lord has blessed in other ways, but this particular problem seems insoluble.

"I've started tithing regularly in the last few weeks, but that doesn't seem to have made any difference either."

I wondered, "What does this man expect in a few weeks of tithing—miracles? Doesn't he have any patience?" That's what I was thinking until I turned to the next sheet. It was a second letter, and had been enclosed in the same envelope.
"Russ,

"I wrote the first message in a fit of discouragement. Since then, in the last few days...we now have a car! Praise the Lord! Our faith is increased because the Lord met our need.

"P.S. The Lord restrained me from sending the first letter."

I began to laugh and praise God when I read the second letter. Interwoven with the Lord's loving and faithful ways is a delightful heavenly sense of humor.

"And if you obey the voice of the Lord your God, being careful to do all His commandments... the Lord will command the blessing upon you in your barns, and in all that you undertake..." (Deuteronomy 28:1,8).

The tithe is not a request of the Lord; it's a command. The perfect illustration was shared by our good friend, Lutheran evangelist Herbert Mjorud.

Herb's cousin is a farmer's wife. Her husband was crippled—confined to a wheelchair—and she had been running the farm. The two had recently made a commitment to the Lord, and part of that commitment was that they were going to give a tithe of the farm's income to the work of the Lord.

Some months later, she began to develop arthritis in her fingers. The pain was increasing. So one day, as she was milking the cows, she prayed, "Lord, I don't understand. My husband and I made a full commitment of our lives to you. How can we survive with my husband crippled and me with arthritis in my fingers?"

She heard a still, small voice in her heart: "The tithe."

"But Lord," she protested. "We are tithing...I think..." By this time she wasn't certain. So when the milking was finished, she went to the house and got out the checkbook. To her surprise, she discovered that they had slowly dropped down and down from the ten percent level of giving to their Lutheran church.

She went to the bank that week—after totalling the shortage—and withdrew more than two hundred dollars. Placing the money in her church offering envelope, she sealed it and drove to the Sunday morning service.

The offering plates were passed, and she presented the envelope containing the full amount needed to bring the tithe current. As the envelope dropped in the offering plate, the arthritis left her fingers!

"You shall serve the Lord your God, and I will bless your bread and your water; and I will take sickness away from the midst of you" (Exodus 23:25).

I've never allowed the spirit of poverty to affect my personal finances since that glorious deliverance many years ago. For five or six years prior to my receiving a salary from the Christian TV station, I was "on my own." God had so thoroughly freed me from the fear of personal poverty that I could easily give up my pastor's salary. When the Lord instructed me to resign as pastor of the Pittsburgh Church of the Brethren in 1972, I had only a vague idea of how my income might be supplied. Yet I wasn't worried in the least; God had told me to resign. It also meant that I had to move out of the security of a parsonage and buy our first home with little money in sight. God gave me a new career; I became a writer and an evangelist.

As the word spread through the church that we needed a down payment on a home, folks began giving us five or ten dollars at a time. I suddenly received a lot of invitations for speaking engagements. God worked a financial miracle in the purchase of our home—a very personal, tailor-made miracle. I wish I could share the full, very intimate story, but let it be sufficient to say that it was spectacular—a sovereign work of God's grace. He gave us a home we could never have afforded under normal circumstances. Then I withdrew the retirement funds our denomination was holding for me, added it all up, and made the down payment, and had fourteen dollars left over! I had resigned with very little money available, but in His providence God gave us a home.

I knew—I just knew!—that we had no reason to fear for our financial security. The Lord had it all in His hands! I even offered to continue as pastor of the Church until my replacement came five months later—without salary. And so I did! We were—with our three children who were still at home—off to a financial adventure with Jesus!

My weekly income varied wildly, up and down. Yet, at the end of each of those five or six years, I always seemed to have earned slightly more than the year before—just enough to take care of the cost of inflation.

Chapter 5

God Does the Impossible

"It depends on faith...in the God who...calls into existence the things that do not exist" (Romans 4:16,17).

In 1969, God gave Norma a vision for a Christian television station in Pittsburgh. She protested, "But Lord, where will we get the money?" He assured her that the money was there, and that He had faithful people through whom He would provide it.

I wondered why God picked Norma and me. After all, we didn't know anything about television stations. Today I realize that He chose the right two people to be a part of the miracle. As I said, Norma and I knew nothing about television. And that's the key. We were not aware that building a TV station with no money was an impossibility. So that's how we were able to do it: we didn't know it couldn't be done! Therefore, we could trust the Holy Spirit to do the building.

Contributions began to come in, soon at the rate of about $3,500 each month. This was nice, but not nearly enough to build a TV station. That's all we were receiving for several years—long, discouraging years. Finally, I prayed, "Lord, if you don't do something to provide enough money to build this TV station—I quit!"

At the same time, our Board of Directors felt led to tithe the ministry's income, even as small as it was. One-tenth would be given to other Christian works. We didn't realize it at the time, but this is a command of God for those who are in full-time service to the Lord. Only long after did we discover from the Bible that it is quite scriptural for a Christian ministry to give a tenth of its income to other ministries. The Bible calls it "a tithe of the tithe."

In Numbers 18 God says that the Levites, who were to be supported financially by the tithes of the rest of Israel, were to give to the priests one-tenth of the tithes they received from the people. The priests were the other group in full-time service to the Lord.

"You shall say to the Levites, 'When you take from the people of Israel the tithe which I have given you from them for your inheritance, then you shall present an offering from it to the Lord, a tithe of the tithe'" (Numbers 18:26).

And so, in the spring of 1976, we began to share our

tiny tithe with other Christian ministries.

A few weeks later, the Greater Pittsburgh Charismatic Conference was held at Duquesne University. Loren Cunningham, founder of *Youth with a Mission*, was to be the Saturday evening speaker. Early in the week, Loren told Norma that the Lord had spoken to him as he was praying about his Saturday message. "God told me that some Christians in Pittsburgh were planning to build a television station, and He said that I am to take an offering for this project on Saturday night." He was thrilled as Norma assured him that God had indeed ordained a Christian TV station and that I was leading the television project. He challenged the folks in his message on Saturday, and nearly $25,000 was received in cash and pledges!

Soon thereafter, I received a letter from some friends who said they had made a covenant with God: "Lord, if you will sell our property for $150,000, we will give the tithe to the Christian TV station project." Enclosed with the letter was a check for $15,000! The property had been sold to the first person who looked at it—with no haggling over the price.

Our Board of Directors was discussing how we might publicize our need for funds. "How about a telethon on Channel 53?" "Oh, they'd never agree to that!" "Well, maybe they would." "At any rate, it won't hurt to ask."

So we asked, and, amazingly, the owners of

Channel 53 agreed. We were astonished. They allowed us to purchase time throughout one weekend for a telethon to build our TV station.

The Board of Directors looked at each other: "Now that we have permission, who knows anything about a telethon?"

Nobody. So we asked the PTL Club if we could come to North Carolina to find out how to conduct a telethon. Two of us flew to Charlotte and met with the young men who directed their telethons. Then we went into the studio to watch the PTL Club as it was being produced.

Jim Bakker recognized me in the audience. Immediately, the Holy Spirit told Jim to take up an offering on the PTL Club for the new TV station in Pittsburgh. Jim spent a good deal of the program asking every viewer to send one dollar to us. "I never heard the Lord speak to me more clearly!" Jim exclaimed.

We received between forty and fifty thousand one dollar bills! And they came from every state in the nation. The money continued to flow as that program was repeated in other cities.

Within three months—with the help of the telethon on Channel 53—the Lord raised our level of income to about $20,000 each month. And it stayed there throughout the construction period. God sent us off to a flying start.

But, shortly after all those blessings, we began to experience a series of tragedies. These terrible disasters included some vicious personal attacks on my integrity, a lawsuit in Federal Court, a petition against us at the Federal Communications Commission, a terrible fire less than two months before our on-air date, and many other lesser problems. We really came face-to-face with the devil.

All these disasters had an effect on my trust in God. Up to that time I had experienced only God's faithfulness. But I began to wonder what terrible thing could happen next. I saw other Christian television ministries prospering while we were suffering through tragedies. Slowly, I began to doubt God's promises concerning Christian television. I became a Christian on the defensive, waiting for the next blow. I was losing a lot of the faith that had enabled me to provide the leadership for other exciting projects that God had instructed me to initiate.

Yet in my personal ministry both at home and overseas, I was watching God perform even greater miracles, some that still inspire awe in me as I recall those mighty acts of God. And throughout those years, Norma and I remained personally free from the spirit of poverty.

But I was quite defensive concerning the vision God had given me for a Christian TV station. I was haunted by fears, wondering what the devil would do to the television project next. Jesus tried to encourage us in Matthew 16: "The gates of Hades shall not prevail against the church." This means that as Christians we have the power to kick in even the very strongholds of death itself. But the scripture seemed to be reversed: I was almost afraid that death would kick in the gates of the TV station. That series of tragedies took its toll on my faith. I lost something during that period; I had serious reservations in my spirit about whether I could still believe God to fulfill His promises about the television station, although I was experiencing so many glorious miracles in my personal ministry.

Finally WPCB-TV, Channel 40, staggered on the air in April 1979. That's right—staggered. Without Norma's prayer group, we wouldn't have made it. At the last moment, the aural controls on our transmitter quit working just four hours before the announced air time, and we were an hour-and-a-half late. Even then, the Lord worked a miracle to put TV40 on the air!

But additional difficulties arose. The expected surge of contributions never materialized. A new problem cropped up, one I'd never anticipated. Many of the cable systems refused to carry our station, WPCB-TV. Some of the cable systems that did carry us placed our Channel 40 on their "garbage" channels. Those are the same channels used by powerful VHF stations; in Pittsburgh they are channels 2, 4, 11 and 13. Thus, on some home TV sets, there is a shadow of the "live" signal competing with our own WPCB-TV. It makes for unpleasant viewing. We have prayed; customers have protested to the cable systems; and we have lodged several legal complaints at the Federal Communications Commission for cable violations. Praise God for the many that have been corrected! Still, a number of problems are not resolved. The FCC has not been enforcing the cable rules.

But that's not the main point of this book. Although some of the cable systems were hurting WPCB-TV financially by their illegal practices, this was not our primary problem. At the time of our on-air date in 1979 the nation's economy was weakening; recession was beginning to set in. And just as we were coming on the air with Channel 40! For the first two years we struggled terribly to do the job with severely limited finances. And that brings me to the real point.

Whenever a friend would inquire about TV40's finances, I would usually try to say an encouraging word. But somehow in the conversation, I would often inject, "Well, we are short of money right now, but the economy is rather weak, you know." I made excuses like that for two years, blaming our shortages on "the recession." I prayed and prayed. All of TV40's people prayed with me. Still, some of our bills were more than a year overdue.

During the summer of 1981, after I had excused TV40's financial plight for the umpteenth time, the Spirit of God spoke—in my spirit. "You blame TV40's shortage of money on the economy. The economy is not your provider! I am! And as long as you *look* to the economy, TV40's finances will *fluctuate* with the economy."

The Lord was right—as always. I felt so foolish, especially since I should have known better. I went over and over the Lord's words in my mind: "The economy is not your provider! I am!"

Almost the same words He had spoken about my personal finances years ago! I had allowed my thinking about TV40's finances to degenerate into "the natural," somehow assuming that the economy is more powerful than God. Not that we weren't praying: we prayed a lot. But when the response wasn't forthcoming, we blamed the nation's financial situation. I observed too that many other Christian television ministries were falling into the same trap—blaming their financial problems on the economy. They were all suffering, too.

I asked God to forgive me. And immediately I told our staff at TV40 that I had a special message for them at our daily prayer meeting. I shared with our folks how God had spoken to me, and I gave an order: "From now on I don't want to hear anybody blaming our financial problems on the economy! God is Jehovah-Jireh—our Provider!" After that we often sang that praise chorus, "Jehovah-Jireh," in our TV40 prayer meetings, for those King James words mean, "The Lord will provide" (Genesis 22:14).

During this period, TV40 had some close calls

with our finances. The electric power was almost shut off one time. After the Lord spoke to me, we went through another financial crisis. But we continued to look to the Lord to provide. It isn't easy to "clean up your language" when you've been talking negatively for a long time.

A few weeks later, I drove to South Carolina for several speaking engagements. I thought I would stop by the PTL Club in Charlotte on the way home. After watching the Jim Bakker program, I walked up to greet Jim and give him a gift. At that time the PTL Television Network was experiencing financial difficulties also. We had scraped together $400 at Channel 40 to make at least a nominal contribution to let Jim Bakker know that we cared.

Jim recognized me from across the stage. He started running and, throwing his arms around me, announced happily, "Russ! The Lord just told me to give you $100,000!"

I was speechless! Rather awkwardly I offered Jim the TV40 check for $400, and he accepted it most graciously.

One hundred thousand dollars! Jim Bakker said the Lord had told him to begin helping other Christian ministries, and TV40 was an early recipient. Jim is a very "giving" person. But that great gift was so supernatural! As soon as Jim had recognized me, the Lord spoke to him to give us that precise amount: $100,000. My knees were almost like water. This occurred only weeks after I quit blaming the economy for TV40's financial problems.

I took the $100,000 PTL Club check with me in the car, planning to surprise our Board of Directors who were to meet on my first day back in Pittsburgh. The Lord very clearly told me to hand it to our Finance Director, Bill Hopper. Bill had been struggling so unsuccessfully to pay the bills. After his presentation of the gloomy financial report to the Board of Directors, I laid the check in front of Bill. When he realized what he was looking at, Bill's body began to shake. The grief of months of seemingly fruitless struggle came out in great sobs. The rest of us began to wipe our eyes, and to praise the Lord with breaking voices.

I passed the $100,000 check around the staff prayer meeting in the afternoon. Everyone was thrilled, and the meeting rang with praises. Bill Hopper began to testify. Tearfully he told everyone how he and his wife had decided at two a.m. the night before that he should resign from TV40: "I just realized that I couldn't put it all together." God, we discovered again, is the Lord of 11:59 p.m. That is God's minute. It's the "miracle minute!" Only faith can keep us walking with Jesus one minute before disaster.

Bill was so blessed as he paid all the old bills. He reminded me of a little boy on Christmas morning. Perhaps the greatest blessing was that every one of TV40's employees realized anew that God's hand is on this ministry. And I recognized mournfully that my former attitude of blaming our troubles on the economy or the cable systems had been blocking God's sovereign hand of blessing for a long time. Every bill over sixty days old was paid!

I like to let people know how things are at TV40. So many wonderful folks hardly watch any other channel. And they care about our financial condition. So I shared during our GETTING TOGETHER program about the grace of God in Jim Bakker's gift. Everyone I met for the next two weeks commented excitedly about the $100,000 gift.

But that one gift did not mean instant prosperity. All the long overdue bills had been paid, but we still were not current. Many partners apparently thought we had all the money we needed, so they stopped giving for a while. And we started to slip back on our bills again—60 days, then 90 days, and some even further.

Nevertheless, we had learned the secret. God is our source! We had been denying His all-sufficiency by complaining about the economy and the cable systems. Now we knew He would take care of our finances.

Two months later, in November 1981, we enjoyed God's blessings in the greatest annual Telethon TV40 ever had. Remember, too, that this was during what the news people were proclaiming loudly was a bad recession. Unemployment in the Pittsburgh market approached 10%. We began to hear glorious individual testimonies of God's provision for Christians who were out of work. Christians must learn anew that God is our Source. "Seek first His kingdom and His righteousness, and all these things will be yours as well"—the fluctuations in the economy notwithstanding.

Slowly Channel 40's finances began to improve again. By April of 1982 our Board of Directors spent a significant part of the Board meeting in praise: the March statement showed TV40 current on all bills for the first time. Ever! Then we reminded ourselves that many other Christian television ministries were mailing out emergency requests for contributions. And so we praised the Lord some more! All our bills were current even in the middle of a recession! God brought us from disaster to victory, all during a period when the national economy was going the opposite direction. "Thanks be to God, who in Christ always leads us to triumph!" (2 Corinthians 2:14).

Of course, good financial management is a significant aspect. Our General Manager, David Kelton, has many thousands of dollars of requests for badly needed equipment by TV40's engineers—just sitting on his desk, waiting for the money to buy them. We are continuing to trust the Lord to provide the finances for this equipment. In the meantime, God has graciously kept our worn-out engineering equipment operating. I have watched the Lord give great wisdom to our management people as they seek Him for answers to difficult problems. Our engineers are doing a great job, with lots of skill and lots of prayer. We really understand at TV40 what the Bible means when it says that the Israelites' clothing did not wear out in forty years. On his desk David Kelton has a humorous hand stamp with an ink pad handy. It says, "NOT APPROVED! Please re-submit in 90 days for final disapproval!"

The point is this: God expects us to be good stewards of all that He gives us. Good stewardship is an integral part of the whole picture; but far more vital is the Lord's great hand of blessing in our lives and in our ministries.

Chapter 6

Selling Cars in the Woods?

"I...endow with wealth those who love me, and I fill their treasuries" (Proverbs 8:20,21).

I learned a delightful lesson during a ministry trip to Sweden a few years ago. Norma and I were scheduled to speak in a series of two-day meetings in churches across southern Sweden. We had never met the man who arranged our itinerary; it was done through a third party. We learned that this man was a used car dealer! I had been expecting a clergyman to arrange my speaking schedule.

We left our meeting in Malmö, Sweden, to travel to the next city. Our interpreter was driving, and he told us that we would be staying at this used car dealer's home. We reached the city of Markaryd and drove beyond it. We continued out of the city and into Sweden's enormous forestland. The road narrowed, and finally the asphalt ended. We were driving more than a mile on a *dirt road*. At last the forest opened into a large clearing, and we beheld the most beautiful used car lot you'd ever want to see!

But used car lots are found on the main streets of cities! How could this be? Next to the car lot was a lovely, rather expensive home, obviously built with the profits from the business. During our visit, I had an opportunity to learn some things about God's material blessings. I asked our host how he could sell cars in the forest! He said nothing, but merely pointed one finger toward heaven. I had to agree. Only God could sell used cars in the woods!

I also began to notice our host's telephone calls. The telephone rang incessantly. Although I understood no Swedish, I discovered how to discern the subject of each call. If the caller was talking about cars, our host was sober, matter-of-fact. But when the call involved the plans for my meetings, he would get excited and become quite animated. He smiled a lot during those calls. His wife told me that her husband had spent most of his time recently arranging for my meetings. She seemed to understand completely.

During a meal our host asked Norma and me to anoint one of his cars. As he explained, "I used to sell a lot of American-made cars. But then the Swedish government placed a prohibitively-high tax on poor-fuel-consumption cars. That ruined my business in American cars. I managed to get rid of all of them except one Plymouth. I've had it for nearly a year-and-a-half."

I asked, "Do you believe that God will sell that car if we anoint it with oil?"

"Yes, I do." We smiled politely at each other.

So Norma took a little bottle of oil from her purse and, after my reading of the scripture from Isaiah 10:27, "...the yoke will be broken because of the anointing," we went out to see the car. There was a thin layer of dust on it. We poured oil on the hood of that Plymouth and prayed and praised the Lord for selling it. As we walked away, our host told his one employee to wash the car and place it in a prominent place for display. "God is going to sell that car," he told his employee.

Shortly after Norma and I returned home, a letter arrived from our used car dealer-friend in Sweden. Here is what it said.

"Dear brother and sister,

"Your visit enriched our lives very much; we thank the Lord for everything. Here is the answer to your prayer. From the moment you prayed, people got interested in the car. Five persons were really interested in buying the car. Two of them had to fight for it. The person pictured here with the car won the battle (a photograph was attached). Your prayer encouraged us in believing God for more miracles."

I wondered how we could possibly have encouraged him in believing God. Actually, he encouraged us. This used car dealer proved without a doubt the truth of Jesus' instruction: "Seek first

His kingdom and His righteousness, and all these physical needs will be yours as well" (Matthew 6:33). God certainly took care of him!

"I am the Lord your God, who teaches you to profit, who leads you in the way you should go" (Isaiah 48:17).

Having been a pastor myself, I know how strong the temptation is for ministers to look to man instead of God for material needs, especially for money to construct church buildings. A well-known evangelist was discussing this matter of money for churches with a businessman whose company was growing rapidly. This Christian businessman found his assets increasing, and he was seeking counsel about opportunities to give large sums of money for Christian works.

The evangelist promised to pray about some specific projects. However, his excitement about the opportunity to spread all that money around the Kingdom apparently made the evangelist impatient. Such a situation can lead a man to speak impulsively for God even when God remains silent. Soon thereafter this evangelist found himself having lunch with two pastors during an international convention. Both pastors are fulfilling good ministries in different cities, with growing congregations among people of limited incomes. We will call them Pastor A and Pastor B. Both are my personal friends.

While the three men were talking together, the evangelist began to get excited about Pastor A's congregation: "The Lord just spoke to me concerning your needs! A wealthy Christian businessman has asked me to counsel him about investing his fortune in Christian work. I feel impressed to have him give you two million dollars to build your new church!"

Pastor A was thrilled. Pastor B rejoiced with him and waited expectantly for a similar gift. But nothing was forthcoming. Privately, Pastor B complained to the evangelist, "Why didn't you include my work? My needs are greater than his!"

"But brother, the Lord didn't give me a specific word for you."

Pastor B was crushed! When he returned to his hotel room, he fell on the bed in tears. "Lord! Why didn't you speak to the evangelist on my behalf?"

The Holy Spirit answered quickly: "That evangelist is not God! I am!"

As time went on, this wealthy businessman became seriously ill, he earned less money than he expected, and he was unable to fulfill any of the evangelist's commitment. Pastor A in the end endured far more disappointment than Pastor B. Both of them learned painfully to look to God, not man.

Chapter 7

Farmers Know How to
Plant for the Harvest

"The Lord is able to give you much more than this" (2 Chronicles 25:9).

Some years ago I was preaching for several days in a rural congregation. My host was a farmer. He and his family lived on a lovely farm, and he told me a most interesting story about how God had taken him from bankruptcy to prosperity. "One time a number of years ago I needed $20,000 for the farm, and I only had a small portion of that amount available. Actually, I was almost bankrupt. I had no idea of where I would get the rest of the money. As I was praying, I felt led by God to 'tithe my need.'"

I looked at him quizzically. The farmer smiled and went on. "I needed $20,000, so I gave one-tenth of my need, $2,000, to a missionary project. It was my 'seed.' What a thrill it was to see God provide the entire $20,000 when the money was due!

"Although I was virtually bankrupt at the time, I learned the principle of sowing seeds for prosperity. Most of my bills on the farm come in large, irregular amounts. So each time, just before a big payment was due, I would give one-tenth of that amount to the Lord's work. And I have never missed a payment since. I always 'tithe my need' in addition to my regular giving to my church."

This is a biblical principle with an added dimension. The farmer discovered how to expand upon the basic building block of the tithe. He gave further out of a specific need. First, his normal tithe, then an additional tithe based upon the amount of money he needed. God had still more to work with, and so the creative miracle had the possibility of being much greater.

Paul gives us the most complete teaching on planting for prosperity in this manner in Second Corinthians. Read the following carefully.

"The point is this: he who sows sparingly will also reap sparingly, and he who sows bountifully will also reap bountifully. Each one must do as he has made up his mind, not reluctantly or under compulsion, for God loves a cheerful giver. And God is able to provide you with every blessing in abundance, so that you may always have enough of everything and may provide in abundance for every good work....

"He who supplies seed to the sower and bread for food will supply and multiply your resources and increase the harvest of your righteousness. You will

be enriched in every way for great generosity, which overflows in many thanksgivings to God" (2 Corinthians 9:6-8,10-12).

Paul makes this law of prosperity quite clear. *God will bless you financially only if you give Him seed to work with!* Every farmer knows that.

As far as I know, all of God's creative miracles recorded in the Bible were accomplished when *He started with something.* 2 Peter 3:5 tells us that the "earth was formed out of water"—referring back to the creation of Genesis 1. God always starts with some "seed," like a divine Farmer. For example, the Sidonian widow offered Elijah only a handful of meal and a little oil, yet the food lasted for more than two years. Elisha befriended the widow of one of his student-prophets by asking God to multiply her tiny supply of oil. On to the New Testament, Jesus never performed a creative miracle out of nothing. He placed mud on less-than-whole eyeballs to produce two complete eyes. He made wine out of water. He fed 5,000 after beginning with five loaves of bread and two fish. In Matthew 15:30,31, people with missing hands or feet found to their joy that new ones had grown out of their stumps.

As you can see, a creative miracle seems to require some material to begin with—a seed, if you will. So, if you need a creative miracle of prosperity, be a good farmer and give God some seed to work with, a portion of prosperity which He can multiply.

Obviously, it is a biblical truth that God will not create a miracle when nothing is made available for His Spirit to work with, or multiply. Certainly, Almighty God *could* make something out of nothing, but the Bible gives clear testimony that He has chosen not to do so.

Abraham offered something very precious— his own son Isaac—as a sacrifice (Genesis 22). Then God could provide a more appropriate sacrifice, a ram whose horns were caught in a thicket. "So Abraham called the name of the place 'Jehovah-Jireh,' which means 'The Lord will provide'" (Genesis 22:14).

Even when we consider the resurrection from the dead, Paul says in 1 Corinthians 15 that "What you sow does not come to life unless it dies....God gives it a body as He has chosen....It is sown in weakness, it is raised in power." So, although one body is physical and the other spiritual, our glorious resurrection bodies will be somehow a continuation, a multiplication, a transformation from the physical-emotional-spiritual persons we are now. We will be recognizable as the same people, but we'll be so much greater. Simply, our bodies are seeds which must first die to produce the greatest miracle of all.

Of course, this book is dealing with physical needs, particularly in the area of finances. *The tithe is the basic seed* from which God can bring forth creative financial miracles. The tithe is the building block of prosperity. I know a Christian whose income for a period of time was only ten dollars a week, yet he faithfully gave one dollar to his church every Sunday. His testimony of God's provision during those months was nothing short of spectacular!

"He who regards the clouds will not reap" (Ecclesiastes 10:4).

What about those Christians who abuse the principles of God's provision? Planting little or no seed, they expect a gold coin in the mouth of every fish. These biblical principles of course give God's people no license to loaf. Please do not misunderstand the message of this book. There is the occasional Christian who would love to "do the Lord's work" while ignoring his family's physical needs. Lazy or irresponsible people will often misinterpret Matthew 6:33 to suit their own purposes. God will not honor us when we twist His Word. Likewise, malingerers and hypochondriacs seldom receive divine healing for their many "ailments." The Word of God has some stern instructions on the subject of church members not doing an honest day's work.

"...Keep away from any brother who is living in idleness....If anyone will not work, let him not eat. For we hear that some of you are living in idleness,

mere busybodies, not doing any work. Now such persons we command and exhort in the Lord Jesus Christ to do their work in quietness and to earn their own living" (2 Thessalonians 3:6,10-12).

This sounds rather foreign to America's standards nowadays, but it's the Word of God! You and I are commanded by the Lord to work hard.

"And whatever you do, in word or deed, do everything in the name of the Lord Jesus, giving thanks to God the Father through Him" (Colossians 3:17).

In many nations there are people who work hard, yet still live in poverty. This is because they have not known the God and Father of our Lord Jesus Christ, the One who blesses our human labor and prospers our efforts to earn a living. Most Americans who are prosperous today are direct descendants of God-fearing, hard-working people. It would be wise for every well-to-do American to remind himself daily of this important scripture from Deuteronomy:

"You shall remember the Lord your God, for it is He who gives you power to get wealth" (Deuteronomy 8:18).

Christians and Jews are the only ones who know this secret.

"You have sown much, and harvested little; you eat, but you never have enough; you drink but you never have your fill; you clothe yourselves, but no one is warm; and he who earns wages earns wages to put them into a bag with holes" (Haggai 1:6).

There are those in our world who have gained a great deal of wealth by unethical and dishonest means. The Bible repeatedly describes how temporary such prosperity will be. "Wealth hastily gotten will dwindle..." (Proverbs 13:11). Even Arab oil sheiks are going to lose everything they have. Only those who honor the one true God will enjoy putting their earnings into bags without holes. "An inheritance gotten hastily in the beginning will in the end not be blessed" (Proverbs 20:21).

"Give, and it will be given unto you; good measure, pressed down, shaken together, running over, will be put into your lap. For the measure you give will be the measure you get back" (Luke 6:38).

Norma was complaining to the Lord one time, many years ago, about "Russell's ways with money." "Lord, aren't we ever going to have some nice things like other people?"

The Lord responded to Norma gently: "Don't ever expect to have many 'things.' If Russell receives more money than he needs, he will only give it away. But that is the way I created him. I will take care of your needs." Norma has been satisfied ever since that assuring word from the Lord. Although she disagrees on rare occasions, Norma seldom questions a financial decision I have made. But I have learned that Norma hears from the Lord more often than I, so I ask her to pray with me about some of the gifts I feel we should be making to particular areas of God's work.

Today Norma and I live almost as simply as we did twenty years ago. Norma still loves a bargain when shopping; and the only reason we buy extra clothes is because we are expected to look good on television and in the churches where I speak. As Norma has time, she enjoys sewing a new article of clothing for herself. The financial striving, the keeping-up-with-the-Joneses, the envying of others who have more "things," the insecurity about our future finances—such matters do not concern us. The Lord made us content when He delivered Norma and me from the spirit of poverty. We are both determined that we will not fall into the trap of affluence that has ensnared a few of America's evangelists.

Pat Robertson has helped me on this matter, and I don't even think he is even aware of his ministry to me. I observed more than twelve years ago when I first met Pat that he accepted no salary from the Christian Broadcasting Network. He would wear bargain suits, even go on television with a hole in his shoe. He genuinely did not care. Yet Pat is the son of a United States senator! Only at the insistence of his associates at CBN has Pat finally accepted a salary and bought some more expensive clothes. To Pat Robertson the ministry of CBN is of paramount importance. I like that, and I think Jesus does, too.

Chapter 8

Look Up for Provision

"Before Him no creature is hidden, but all are open and laid bare to the eyes of Him with whom we have to do" (Hebrews 4:13).

The world around us wants us to believe that earthly forces are determinative for our lives. "Forget about all that 'pie in the sky' religion, and face reality!" That's what the world is saying to us.

On the contrary, it is *God* "with whom we have to do." So does the rest of the world, although they don't want to admit it. "The mills of God may grind slowly, but they grind exceedingly fine." So goes an old proverb that is alive with truth. The rest of the world will realize it some day, tragically too late for many of them.

"The earth has yielded its increase; God, our God, has blessed us" (Psalms 67:6).

We who are Christians—knowing that the

Lord God is our Provider—should be pondering, thinking about, meditating on, and feeding from, His written Word. Stop fretting about the fluctuations of the economy. Especially you should ignore what the news media are saying. They will take your attention from your true Provider and cause you to worry about the government.

I write particularly to those elderly Christians who are receiving Social Security checks each month, those who remember so clearly the Depression of the 1930's. The media are attempting to panic everyone who is suffering from the spirit of poverty. Do not be troubled about the alarms being publicized on television and in the newspapers. The people sounding these alarms about Social Security are not really interested in you: they merely want to *use* you to gain their own political advantage. *God* is the only One who truly cares about you.

"So shall my word be that goes forth from my mouth; it shall not return to me empty, but it shall accomplish that which I purpose, and prosper in the thing for which I sent it" (Isaiah 55:11).

If you are having financial difficulties—and even if you aren't—spend time occasionally to feed your mind on the scriptures scattered throughout this book. They will slowly but surely build your faith. *The Word of God works!* Now feed on it!

"If they hearken and serve him, they complete their days in prosperity, and their years in pleasantness" (Job 36:11).

"And my God will supply every need of yours according to his riches in glory in Christ Jesus" (Philippians 4:19).

"This book of the law shall not depart out of your mouth, but you shall meditate on it day and night, that you may be careful to do according to all that is written in it; for then you shall make your way prosperous, and then you shall have good success" (Joshua 1:8).

"Take delight in the Lord, and he will give you the desires of your heart....I have been young, and now am old; yet I have not seen the righteous forsaken or his children begging bread" (Psalms 37:4,25).

"O fear the Lord, you his saints, for those who fear him have no want!...But those who seek the Lord lack no good thing" (Psalms 34:9,10).

Now pray this prayer—out loud. Pray it only if you mean it. There is nothing magical about it. God knows your heart, and He is always faithful. Pray it calmly, with no anxiety, accepting only a sense of quiet excitement about what the Lord is preparing to do for you.

"Father, I give my life to you. Forgive me for my sin of doubting you. Especially now I deliberately give you my finances. I present to you all of my physical needs—food, home, clothes, job, taxes— every thing! I praise you for being Jehovah-Jireh, my Provider.

"I will not worry about my finances again. I will tithe to your work. I will never again complain about high prices; nor will I complain about my income. I will have no anxiety about anything, but in everything by prayer and supplication with thanksgiving, I will let you know of my requests.

"I pray in the name of Jesus Christ. Amen."

Chapter 9

The Greatest Prosperity

"For what will it profit a man, if he gains the whole world and forfeits his life?" (Matthew 16:26).

Having said all this about a Christian and his financial needs, an important word is in order. It is based upon Luke 10:17-21. Jesus sent out seventy disciples, two-by-two, with instructions about preaching, teaching, healing and casting out demons. "The seventy returned with joy, saying, 'Lord, even the demons are subject to us in your name!'"

You and I could add joyously, "Even the demon of *poverty* is subject to us in your name!"

Jesus commended His disciples for their obedience. But He added one of the important words of the New Testament: "Nevertheless, do not rejoice in this, that the spirits are subject to you; but rejoice that your names are written in heaven."

Eternal life is the greatest miracle! All the wealth of this world could never equal the wealth

God has reserved for even the least one among His children! For we are co-heirs with Jesus Christ of all the prosperity and glory and joy and love of our Father's Kingdom! It's ours, and it's free! It's been paid for by the life-blood of our Lord Jesus Christ! How trivial are our earthly needs!

Yet God cares even about those physical needs. He notices each hair that falls from your head. This book points up God's concern for every one of these trivial matters. So let's keep our vision in proper perspective. A word from C. S. Lewis sums it up: "Aim at heaven and you will get earth 'thrown in': aim at earth and you will get neither."*

"Rejoice that your names are written in heaven."

* C. S. Lewis, *Mere Christianity*, N.Y., MacMillan, 1960, p.118.

About the Author

Russell Bixler spent seven years in the business world after he received his bachelor's and master's degrees. His plans to go on to law school were derailed when God called him into the ministry. He went to seminary, and, when his theological studies were complete, he was called to the pastorate of a Church of the Brethren congregation in Pittsburgh, Pennsylvania.

It was during his thirteen years at the Church of the Brethren that the callings of God became more and more exciting. Each seemed to be a little more impossible than the last, but with God *all things* are possible.

In the 1970s the charismatic renewal in the Pittsburgh area was greatly nurtured by the interdenominational prayer meetings held at Russ' church. At the same time, God began to use him in Christian literature: for several years he wrote and edited for three Christian publishers. He also founded and served as Chairman of the Planning Committee for the Greater Pittsburgh Charismatic Conference, which gained international fame.

God spoke to his wife, Norma, and then confirmed with Russ, His will concerning their biggest challenge of all—a Christian television ministry. After a decade of prayer, planning, and faith, on Easter Sunday 1979, WPCB-TV (Channel 40) went on the air. The ministry grew from a small TV station that reached western Pennsylvania, West Virginia, and eastern Ohio, to the 24-hour-a-day broadcast of the Good News of Jesus to the western hemisphere via satellite, and then via live streaming video to computers and handheld devices of all Cornerstone TeleVision Network programs.

Russ Bixler went home to be with the Lord in the year 2000, but the vision God gave him and Norma—of reaching the world for Christ via broadcast media—continues to expand and be carried out around the globe through the faithful efforts of the CTVN ministry team.